Alexander Sturgis

Introducing
Rembrandt

Belitha Press

Rembrandt by Himself

All these pictures are of the same person. Can you tell what sort of man he was? Can you tell what he did?

The man in all these pictures is the subject of this book. His name was Rembrandt. He was an artist who lived and worked over three hundred years ago. The pictures are not only of him but they are by him as well.

Looking at these portraits you might not realize that you were looking at pictures of a painter. Rembrandt often painted himself in fancy dress or as a rich man-about-town rather than in a painter's apron holding a paintbrush. Perhaps this was because he wanted people to think of him as a wealthy gentleman rather than as a simple artist.

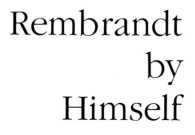

Self-portrait, painting, aged twenty-three (left).

Self-portrait, etching, aged twenty-four (right top).

Self-portrait, etching, aged thirty-three (right middle).

Self-portrait, etching, aged twenty-four (right bottom).

Rembrandt did not write about his life but in these pictures he tells us a great deal about himself. Looking at these self-portraits we can see him growing from a young twenty-three-year-old into an old man of sixty-three. Did he change with age? Was he proud? Was he successful? Did he have a happy life?

After you have read more about Rembrandt you can look at these portraits again and see if your ideas have changed.

*Self-portrait, painting,
aged fifty-one (right).*

*Self-portrait, painting,
aged sixty-three (below).*

Early Years

Rembrandt is one of the few men or women in history recognizable from just his first name. Others are Napoleon, Leonardo and Cleopatra. Rembrandt's full name was Rembrandt Harmenszoon van Rijn. His surname, Van Rijn, means 'from the Rhine'. The Rhine is one of the great rivers of Europe. Rembrandt was born in 1606 at Leiden in Holland near where the river finally reaches the sea. His father, Harmen, was a miller who owned a windmill outside the city walls that ground malt for making beer.

Rembrandt went to school until he was thirteen, when he left because he wanted to learn to be a painter. Although this seems young, most boys at that time left school when they were ten, and most girls did not go to school at all.

Constantin Huygens saw this painting when he visited the young Rembrandt's studio. He thought it was brilliant and described the figure of Judas as 'demented, wailing . . . with an awful face, torn hair, clothes torn to shreds, twisted limbs and hands clenched so hard they bleed.'
The Repentant Judas, 1629.

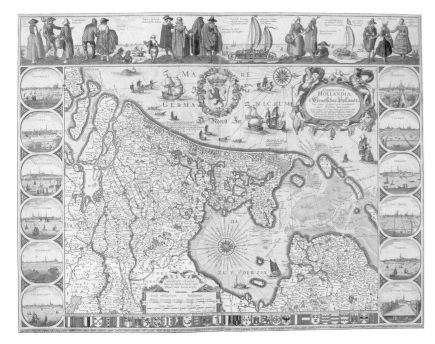

This Dutch map of 1606 shows Rembrandt's birthplace of Leiden. The old map has been drawn at a strange angle. The correct position of the Netherlands is shown above.

Rembrandt started learning to be a painter by becoming a painter's apprentice (see illustration on page 14). As an apprentice Rembrandt did all kinds of odd jobs around the artist's studio such as mixing paints and cleaning brushes as well as learning to paint. After studying in Leiden for three years Rembrandt finished his training with a painter called Pieter Lastman (1583-1633) in Amsterdam.

Rembrandt was now seventeen and he returned to his home town as a fully trained painter. Together with another young painter called Jan Lievens (1607-74) he started his own studio. A visitor to the studio was amazed by the work of the two young artists. 'Never have I come across such hard work and dedication,' he wrote. The visitor, Constantin Huygens, was an important man himself. He was looking for artists to paint pictures for the palaces of the Dutch leader Prince Frederick Henry. When he saw Rembrandt's work he was sure he had found just the man.

Constantin Huygens was one of the first men to recognize Rembrandt's genius.
Constantin Huygens and his Clerk, by Thomas de Keyser, 1627.

Holland in the Seventeenth Century

Before Rembrandt's birth, Belgium, Luxembourg and Holland were one country known as the Netherlands. Until 1579 the Netherlands were ruled by the king of Spain, but in this year the country was split in two. The southern part of the country stayed under Spanish rule, and the northern part of the Netherlands – which we now call Holland – broke away to rule themselves. The new country was made up of seven of the seventeen provinces (regions or counties) that had made up the Netherlands, and was known as the United Provinces or the Dutch Republic. A republic is a country without a king or queen that governs itself. Although there was no king

This is a map of Europe of 1630. The red arrow points to the Netherlands.

The enormous town hall of Amsterdam, at the back of this painting, was started in 1648 and filled with paintings and sculpture by the artists of the city. Rembrandt created a huge painting for the town hall of which only a part survives (see page 26).
Dam Square, Amsterdam, by Jacob van der Ulft, 1659.

of the Dutch Republic they did have a leader called the Stadtholder. In Rembrandt's time this leader was Prince Frederick Henry.

The new country was an exciting place for painters. Prince Frederick built palaces which had to be decorated with pictures. In the cities the new rulers built town halls which they also filled with art works. But it was not just the rulers of the Dutch Republic who bought pictures. Visitors to Holland from England were amazed by the number of pictures ordinary people had in their homes. The visitors commented that they had never seen a country that loved art more.

Here, the Dutch leader of Rembrandt's time is shown wearing armour. One of his most important tasks was to lead the Dutch army against the Spanish, from whom the Dutch won their independence.
Prince Frederick Henry, by Gerard van Honthorst, 1631.

Portraits — Painting People

The Anatomy Lesson of Dr Tulp of 1632, was a very important picture in Rembrandt's career. There were no public museums in Rembrandt's time but this painting was hung in the surgeon's meeting hall which people visited so Rembrandt's fame as a portrait painter spread.

When Rembrandt was twenty-five he moved to the city of Amsterdam to continue his work as a painter. He quickly became the leading portrait painter to the rich families of the city. Everybody who was anybody wanted their portrait painted by the young artist and people begged him to paint them.

Rembrandt painted non-stop and finished at least one picture every fortnight, of which about half were portraits. Looking at the portraits on this page you might not realize how rich the people in them were. At this time in Holland

people were worried about showing off their riches and usually dressed in black. But if you look closely you can see that their clothes are not as simple as they seem. They are made of the finest materials (like silk, velvet and lace) and have delicately embroidered patterns on them.

It was not just single people who wanted their portraits painted by Rembrandt. *The Anatomy Lesson of Dr Tulp* (see left), is a portrait of a group. All these men were members of a society of surgeons (like a club). Rembrandt has not painted them in a row like a team photograph but listening to a lecture given by Dr Tulp. Dr Tulp has peeled back the skin of a dead man's arm and is showing his audience the muscles attached to the hand.

We do not know the name of this man (top right) or when he was painted but he was probably an Amsterdam merchant. Oval-shaped portraits were very fashionable at this time and Rembrandt painted large numbers of them.

This is a portrait of a lady called *Agatha Bas*, painted in 1641. Agatha belong to one of Amsterdam's richest families. She wears the finest clothes and is dripping with jewellery. Her thumb sticks out over a painted frame to make us think she is standing at a window.

Amsterdam

When Rembrandt moved to Amsterdam, it was one of the greatest and richest cities in the world. Today, Amsterdam is famous for its canals and flower markets but at the time it was the main port of Europe. Ships from Amsterdam sailed all over the world. They collected grain from Russia and travelled as far as America, Japan and the East and West Indies for more exotic goods such as spices, silk and tobacco. The goods that came into Amsterdam were sold all over Europe, and the businessmen of the city were in charge of all this trading. In America, New York used to be under Dutch control and was even called New Amsterdam.

This modern-day photograph of Amsterdam (left) shows one of the grand merchant's houses built in Rembrandt's day. In front runs one of the city's many canals.

Although he lived in the city for most of his life this is one of the very few pictures that Rembrandt made of Amsterdam (below). You can see the windmills for which Holland is still famous. On the left are the masts of the ships that crowded into Amsterdam's harbour.
View of Amsterdam, 1640.

The merchants of Amsterdam were among the richest in the world. They built themselves grand town houses which they filled with paintings. It is not surprising that Rembrandt decided to move to the big city.

When Rembrandt arrived in Amsterdam he joined the studio of Hendrick van Uylenburgh. Hendrick was more of a businessman than a painter. He bought and sold old paintings as well as having new ones painted. Rembrandt soon became his chief artist. Rembrandt would paint the pictures and Hendrick would sell them. The two men were not just working partners, for in 1634 Rembrandt married Hendrick's cousin Saskia.

Rembrandt the Teacher

This painting of an *Artists Academy* (1656) by the Dutch painter Michiel Sweerts gives us a good idea of what a drawing class was like in Rembrandt's time. Some of the boys seem to be paying much more attention than others.

Rembrandt's success as a painter meant that young artists wanted to come and learn from him. Even experienced artists who had their own studios came to be taught by the master.

The painting above shows a drawing school during Rembrandt's time. The master or head of the studio, in his painter's cap, has his back to us. The young boys draw the naked model who stands in the middle of the room. Look at the three pictures on the right. The print (page 15, bottom right-hand picture) is by Rembrandt, but the two drawings are by his pupils. You can see that they all show the same boy, leaning his elbow on a cushion, but seen from different positions in the room. We can imagine Rembrandt strolling round looking over the shoulders of his pupils, making comments, while they drew the young boy who is posing.

Rembrandt's pupils not only learnt to draw in his studio, they were also taught how to paint like Rembrandt himself. They copied paintings that Rembrandt had made. A person who visited Rembrandt's studio described it as overflowing with pupils. He also complained that Rembrandt would sometimes add his own signature to paintings done by his students and then sell them as if he had painted them himself.

These are the drawings that Rembrandt's pupils made in his studio. The print (bottom right) is by Rembrandt himself and is of the same boy in the same pose. Rembrandt may have made this print and others like it as a model for his pupils to copy and learn from.
Workshop Studies, by Rembrandt and his pupils, 1646.

Painting Stories

In Rembrandt's time a painter could specialize in different types of painting. Rembrandt was famous for his portraits. Other painters produced landscapes or still lifes. Still lifes are pictures of fruit and flowers or domestic objects.

The kind of painting that was thought to be the most important and difficult was called history painting. This meant paintings of stories from the Bible (like the two opposite), from Greek or Roman legends or from history. The painter of stories had to be able to paint people, landscapes (if the stories happened outside) and still lifes as well. In Rembrandt's painting *Belshazzar's Feast* (see top right of page 17) he has painted a still life of grapes and figs on the banqueting table.

Rembrandt's history paintings are very dramatic. He often made them more exciting by painting strong contrasts between the light and dark. The paintings almost look as if they are happening in a theatre under a spotlight.

Rembrandt was famous for being able to paint feelings and emotions. He did this by painting people's faces and expressions but also by the way he painted their bodies. In *Belshazzar's Feast* the king is surprised and frightened by the mysterious writing on the wall. Look at the way Rembrandt has put these feelings into his face and body, he looks horrified and recoils from the hand.

In the painting *The Blinding of Samson* (bottom of page 17) it is not fear but anger and agony that Rembrandt wanted to show. Look at Samson's clenched fists and curled toes. It is these parts of his body rather than his face that tells us the most about how he feels.

Belshazzar, the king of Babylon, held a great feast using the silver and gold cups and plates he had stolen from the Temple in Jerusalem. Suddenly, a mysterious hand appeared and wrote that the Babylonian kingdom would end soon. That night Belshazzar was killed.
Belshazzar's Feast, c.1635.

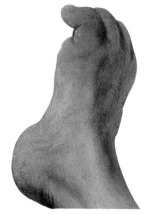

Samson was a man with superhuman strength which came from his long hair. He was tricked by the beautiful Delilah into revealing his secret and while he was asleep she cut off his hair. Samson's enemies, the Philistines, then leapt out and captured him. They blinded Samson and imprisoned him.
The Blinding of Samson, 1636.

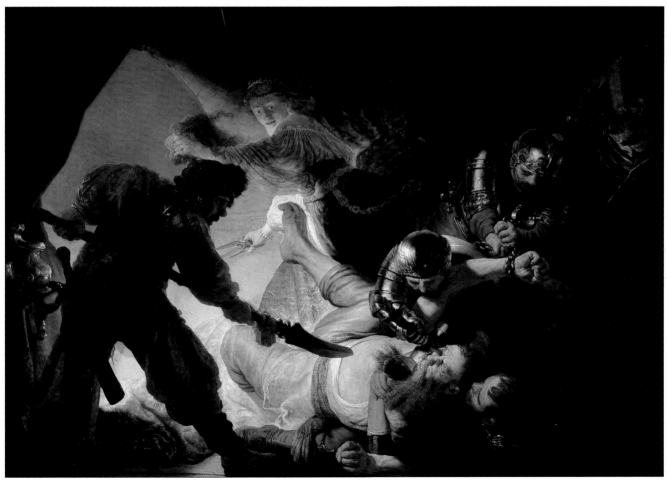

The Night Watch

This is probably Rembrandt's most famous painting. It is known as *The Night Watch*. In fact the title is misleading because the scene is not happening at night – no one has any torches or lanterns – and the people in it are not keeping watch. The picture was first called *The Night Watch* about one hundred and fifty years after it was painted, probably because it had darkened with age and this made it look as if the scene was happening at night.

 This is Rembrandt's eye under his painter's beret. He is staring out of the painting at us. Can you find where this detail comes from? He is next to the flag carrier, called the ensign, at the back of the painting.
The Night Watch, 1642.

The photograph (top right) gives you an idea of the size of *The Night Watch*.

Although the painting looks as if it might be a scene from a battle it is actually a group portrait (see pages 10-11). Sixteen of the people in the painting paid to have their portraits included in the picture. Can you work out which ones they are? The people who were painted at the front would have paid more than those whose faces poke up at the back.

The men in the painting were members of a company of guardsmen. Guardsmen were not proper soldiers but rich townsmen who were allowed to carry weapons. There were probably about two hundred men in the company but only the richest could afford to be put into Rembrandt's painting.

The captain of the guardsmen is the man dressed in black with the red sash around his chest. The second-in-command is the man in yellow with the white sash.

Rembrandt's guardsmen do not look as if they are posing but as if they are preparing for a battle or a procession. The captain looks as if he is giving a command. Other group portraits of guardsmen look much more posed and unexciting. There is a story that the guardsmen who Rembrandt painted were angered by the painting because it was so unusual. But they paid for it and hung it in their hall so it seems unlikely that this is true.

Rembrandt and Women

The women in Rembrandt's life appear in his paintings. Often they are in fancy dress, a character in a story, or themselves.

The writing on this beautiful drawing (left) says that it is of Rembrandt's wife Saskia and was drawn three days after they were engaged when she was twenty-one. There is another picture of Saskia on page 29 where she is dressed as a Roman goddess. But eight years after they were married Saskia died leaving Rembrandt with a nine-month-old son called Titus.

After Saskia's death Rembrandt started a love affair with Titus's nanny, Geertje Dircks. She may be the *Young Woman in Bed* pulling back the curtain to look at something that has caught her eye (see below).

Rembrandt's young wife Saskia (above) wears a floppy hat and holds a flower. You can see the date of 1633 at the end of the writing underneath the drawing.

This *Young Woman in Bed* of 1645, may well be Geertje Dircks whom Rembrandt was to treat so badly. Something has caught the woman's attention and made her pull back the curtain to her bed but we do not know what it is.

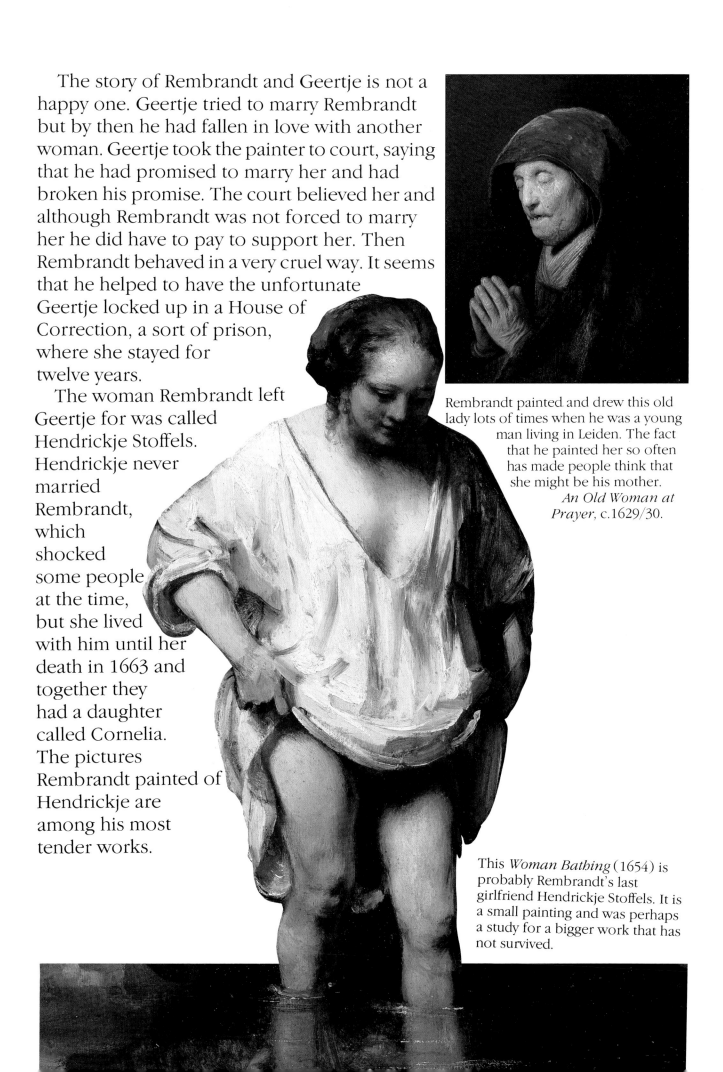

The story of Rembrandt and Geertje is not a happy one. Geertje tried to marry Rembrandt but by then he had fallen in love with another woman. Geertje took the painter to court, saying that he had promised to marry her and had broken his promise. The court believed her and although Rembrandt was not forced to marry her he did have to pay to support her. Then Rembrandt behaved in a very cruel way. It seems that he helped to have the unfortunate Geertje locked up in a House of Correction, a sort of prison, where she stayed for twelve years.

The woman Rembrandt left Geertje for was called Hendrickje Stoffels. Hendrickje never married Rembrandt, which shocked some people at the time, but she lived with him until her death in 1663 and together they had a daughter called Cornelia. The pictures Rembrandt painted of Hendrickje are among his most tender works.

Rembrandt painted and drew this old lady lots of times when he was a young man living in Leiden. The fact that he painted her so often has made people think that she might be his mother.
An Old Woman at Prayer, c.1629/30.

This *Woman Bathing* (1654) is probably Rembrandt's last girlfriend Hendrickje Stoffels. It is a small painting and was perhaps a study for a bigger work that has not survived.

Drawing Bodies

The German artist Albrecht Dürer would have looked at statues like the Roman *Apollo Belvedere* (below) when he made this print of *Adam and Eve* in 1504. Because Dürer's work (right) is a print, which comes out reversed, the legs and arms of Adam have come out the other way round from the statue.

On this page there are two prints of Adam and Eve in the Garden of Eden. One is by Rembrandt (page 23) and the other (above) by an earlier German artist called Albrecht Dürer (1471-1528). Look at the way the two artists have drawn Adam and Eve's bodies. Which do you think is more realistic?

When Dürer made his print he looked at Roman or Greek statues as models for his figures. For Adam, he copied a famous statue of the Roman god Apollo (see left) and for Eve he looked at statues of the Roman goddess of beauty, Venus. His figures, with their smooth, hard bodies, are more like ancient statues than real people.

Rembrandt's Adam and Eve could not look less like statues. You can see the wrinkles in their skin and their rolls of fat. This shocked some people at the time, who were not used to seeing such realistic pictures of naked people, especially people from the Bible. They thought that artists should try and make the bodies of people they painted look like Roman statues. This, they said, was what people should look like even if they did not. One person writing shortly after Rembrandt had died complained about the flabby flesh and old age of the female bodies in his paintings, saying they looked more like washerwomen than goddesses.

Rembrandt would probably have been pleased with this attack. We know he looked at real people such as his relatives and girlfriends when he painted his pictures.

Hand of Belshazzar, see page 17.

Hand of Flora, see page 29.

People in Rembrandt's time not only complained about his paintings of naked bodies, some also said that he could not paint hands properly. Here are two hands from paintings that you can see in this book. Look at the other hands in this book before you decide.

Here is Rembrandt's version of the scene that Dürer had made over one hundred years earlier. As well as making the figures less like statues, Rembrandt has turned the snake into a kind of dragon. *The Fall of Man*, 1638.

23

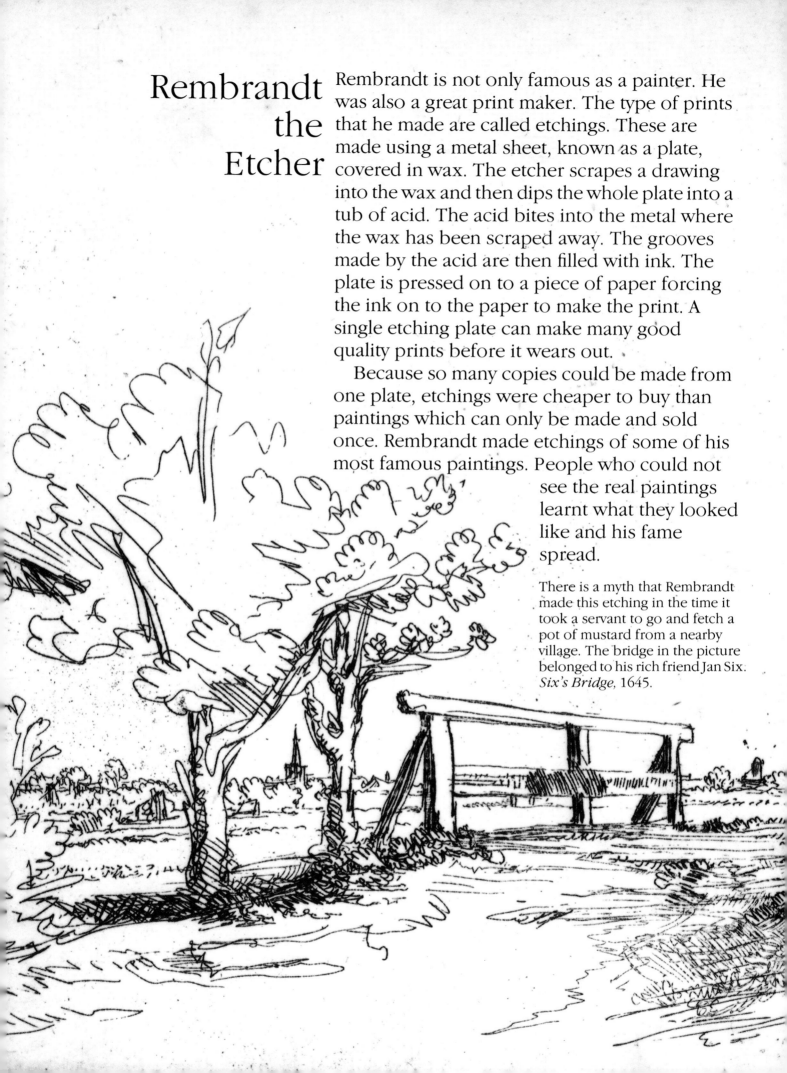

Rembrandt the Etcher

Rembrandt is not only famous as a painter. He was also a great print maker. The type of prints that he made are called etchings. These are made using a metal sheet, known as a plate, covered in wax. The etcher scrapes a drawing into the wax and then dips the whole plate into a tub of acid. The acid bites into the metal where the wax has been scraped away. The grooves made by the acid are then filled with ink. The plate is pressed on to a piece of paper forcing the ink on to the paper to make the print. A single etching plate can make many good quality prints before it wears out.

Because so many copies could be made from one plate, etchings were cheaper to buy than paintings which can only be made and sold once. Rembrandt made etchings of some of his most famous paintings. People who could not see the real paintings learnt what they looked like and his fame spread.

There is a myth that Rembrandt made this etching in the time it took a servant to go and fetch a pot of mustard from a nearby village. The bridge in the picture belonged to his rich friend Jan Six. *Six's Bridge*, 1645.

Rembrandt etched portraits, stories and subjects that he would not have painted, like this pig. People would not have paid a great deal of money for a grand oil painting of a pig. Rembrandt was always experimenting

with his prints. You can see from the examples on this page some of the different effects he could create.

These two etchings of Jesus on the cross were made from the same etching plate. After making the one on the left Rembrandt altered the plate. The second etching is much darker. Some figures have disappeared from the foreground while a man has appeared on a horse in front of the left-hand cross.
The Three Crosses, 1653.

Later Life

After the successes of his early life Rembrandt's old age was full of disappointments and difficulties. Rembrandt seems to have been a difficult man to get on with and he argued with many of the important people who asked him to paint for them. This meant they often did not ask him a second time.

Today, many people think that Rembrandt's later pictures are his greatest works. But during his old age some people saw him as old-fashioned and so preferred the paintings of younger artists.

This was not Rembrandt's only problem. When things were going well Rembrandt spent money as quickly as he earned it. He bought a very expensive house and filled it with a collection of paintings and other art objects. All this was more than Rembrandt could afford and in 1656 he went bankrupt and had to sell his house and all his possessions.

This is all that remains of Rembrandt's huge painting *The Conspiracy of Claudius Civilis* of 1661. Even this fragment is about two metres high. The scene is from Dutch and Roman history. Claudius Civilis, the leader of the Dutch is persuading the other nobles to swear an oath to rise up against their Roman rulers.

Some people did still buy Rembrandt's paintings and near the end of his life he was asked to paint an enormous painting for the new town hall in Amsterdam. Rembrandt must have seen this as a chance to once more prove himself the greatest painter in the city. But things went horribly wrong. The rulers of Amsterdam hated *The Conspiracy of Claudius Civilis* (see bottom of page 26) and removed it from the town hall after only a few months. Today just a small part of the painting survives.

The end of Rembrandt's life was a sad one. Both his girlfriend Hendrickje and his son Titus died before he did leaving him alone with his young daughter Cornelia. Rembrandt finally died on 4 October 1669 at the age of sixty-three.

This young man is possibly Rembrandt's son Titus who died at the age of twenty-seven. Titus learned to be a painter in his father's workshop but no one knows what his paintings looked like or if they have survived.
Portrait of a Young Man, 1668.

This picture was painted the year before Rembrandt was declared bankrupt. It is of an ox's carcass hanging up in a butchers. It is very unlikely that a rich merchant or noble asked him to paint a picture of a dead animal.
Dead Ox, 1655.

How Did He Do It?

Brushes in Rembrandt's time were made of pig's bristles tied on to sticks with string. Soft-haired brushes were made from the fur of stoats and polecats set into pieces of quill from bird's feathers.

The colours Rembrandt used are called earth colours because they are made from different coloured soils ground up with oil.

How did Rembrandt paint the pictures you can see in this book? We do not know exactly but experts have looked long and hard at his paintings to try and discover the secrets of his methods.

Perhaps the best way to discover how Rembrandt painted is to look at one picture in particular. This one is of his wife Saskia dressed as the Roman goddess of flowers (see right). This picture is painted on canvas but Rembrandt also painted on wood and paper. The paint he used was oil paint, made from ground-up colours mixed with an oil, more like cooking oil than oil for a car. The two main differences between oil paint and paints mixed with water are that oil paints are much thicker and they take longer to dry. Rembrandt used these qualities to the full. He would often put the paint on the canvas in great thick lumps, sometimes slapping it on with a knife rather than using a brush. If he was painting hair or fur he would sometimes use the pointed end of his brush to scrape into the paint when it was still wet to make a hair-like effect.

Rembrandt did not always use paint in great blobs. If he was trying to paint a canvas to look smooth like silk or skin he would put the paint on thinly and smoothly. In this way his paintings are often almost like sculptures in paint. This is the most difficult thing to see in a book about paintings by Rembrandt. All the pictures look flat and smooth on the page which is why it is so exciting, and often surprising, to see the real things.

Although this painting of Saskia dressed as the goddess Flora looks flat on the page you can see from the details the different effects Rembrandt could create with oil paints.

This detail of Flora's hair shows where Rembrandt scratched into the surface of the paint with the pointed handle of his paint brush. The hair is in contrast to the smooth painting of the skin.

This detail of Flora's belt shows the great thick blobs of paint Rembrandt used to create the effect of jewel-encrusted gold.

Did He Do It?

The Man in the Golden Helmet (date unknown), once thought to be one of Rembrandt's greatest works, is now believed to be by one of his pupils.

The two pupils of Rembrandt here are Govert Flinck and Carel Fabritius. Both are dressed in ways in which Rembrandt painted himself. Govert Flinck looks so like his master that the painting used to be thought of as a portrait of Rembrandt rather than a self-portrait by Flinck.

A Young Man With a Feathered Cap, by Carel Fabritius (right), 1636.

Self-Portrait, by Govert Flinck (below), 1633.

This painting is known as *The Man With the Golden Helmet.* It is one of Rembrandt's most famous works. Look at it carefully. Many of the things we have seen Rembrandt doing in other paintings in this book are here in this painting. It is a portrait, but also a picture of an expression. The helmet is painted with thick oil paint and there are the dramatic contrasts between light and dark that Rembrandt loved. Many people have thought that this is one of the greatest paintings in the world.

Everything I have just written is true except for one thing. Today, experts say that this picture is not by Rembrandt but by one of his pupils. Look at the picture again. Has it changed? Of course not, but perhaps the way you look at it has.

Because of Rembrandt's fame and success many artists tried to copy his style of painting. Rembrandt taught his pupils to paint exactly like him. They copied his paintings and then painted their own in his style. Many of Rembrandt's pupils even dressed like him and painted themselves looking like their master. These paintings are all self-portraits by Rembrandt's pupils. You can compare them with those by Rembrandt at the beginning of the book.